Memory's Blue Sedan

HYSTERICAL BOOKS

Memory's Blue Sedan

Jesse Millner

HYSTERICAL BOOKS
TALLAHASSEE, FL 2020

Copyright © Jesse Millner 2020
All rights reserved under
International and Pan-American Copyright Conventions.

No portion of this book may be reproduced in any form without the written permission of the publisher, except by a reviewer, who may quote brief passages in connection with a review for a magazine or newspaper.

Memory's Blue Sedan by Jesse Millner — First Edition

Cover image: Sharon Isern
Design, production: Jay Snodgrass
Type Styles:

ISBN — 978-0-940821-15-6
Library of Congress Cataloging Card Number —2020932110

Hysterical Books is dedicated wholly to the publication and appreciation of fine poetry and other literary genres.

HYSTERICAL BOOKS
1506 Wekewa Nene
Tallahassee, Florida

Published in the United States by Hysterical Books
Tallahassee, Florida • First Edition, 2019
hystericalbooks.com
hystericalbooks@gmail.com

For Lyn

Part I: Memory's Blue Sedan

3	How a Single Word
4	Remembering a Palace of Shudders and Sighs
6	Definitions
8	It Spoke Something Beautiful
9	Last Will and Testament: Richmond, Virginia 1863
11	Birthright
13	The Map
15	Every Whispered Word
16	Imagining Sweden
17	A Sky Language
20	Last night, two years after your death, Mom,
21	What the Man Dreams
23	Coronado
24	Why My Porn Name is Gus Lineberry
25	All the Ways I Have Sinned
27	All the Sorrow
28	All the Troubles
30	1968
32	The Past
34	One World at a Time
36	The Light of Other Days
37	At Last, Heaven
39	Memory's Blue Sedan
41	Until I was a Direction

Part II: Confluence

44	Confluence
46	Child of the Corn!
48	I'd Rather be a Cowboy

50	After reading Phil Levine,
51	Here's a Leap
52	I believe in compassion
53	Out of the Midst of the Fire
55	My Heart
57	My First Marriage Compared to the Lewis and Clark Expedition

Part III: Modern Life

62	At a supermarket in South Florida,
64	When the cashier at the grocery asks me
65	Hairdresser of the Dead
66	Instruction
67	How to Keep the Devil Away:
68	Each morning I wake up filled with dreams
70	These days
72	What Do Men Want? After Kim Addonizio
74	The likelihood of death
75	Real Reality
76	During my dark city days
78	Singing to the Night Birds for Michael Hettich
79	I Want to Come Back as a Toaster
80	Because Frank Fell Down
82	Broken World
84	Kudzu Hymn
86	Modern Life
88	Noonday *Duende*
89	Minus
91	Beer Aisle Meditation: Fort Myers, Florida 2018
93	In memory's blue sedan,

Acknowledgements

"Definitions": *The Poydras Review*, Winter 2012; "Last Will and Testament": *Real South Magazine*, June 2013; "How a Single Word": *Foliate Oak*, Fall 2014; "Every Whispered Word," "Imagining Sweden," and "Child of the Corn!": *Northwind*, Fall 2012; "At Last Heaven": *The Four Ties Review*, Fall 2012; "Confluence": *The Florida Review*, Winter 2015; "Noonday Duende": *Squalorly*, January 2014; "I'd Rather be a Cowboy": *upstreet*, August 2012; "Hairdresser of the Dead": *Wraparound South*, Winter 2015; "At a Supermarket in South Florida" and "I have been way too careful with my poems": *Apeiron Review*, Fall 2014; "The Past": *JuxtaProse*, Summer 2015; "It Spoke Something Beautiful," *Lingerpost*, Summer 2016; "1968" and "Because Frank Fell Down": *The Magnolia Review*, Fall 2016; "Two years after your death, mom": *West Texas Literary Review*, Fall 2016; "After Reading Phil Levine": *Steam Ticket*, Spring 2017; "The Map": *Flying South*, Fall 2017; "One World at a Time": *The Comstock Review*, Fall 2017; "My Heart": *Imitation Fruit*, Fall 2017; "Real Reality": *The Split Rock Review*, Fall 2017; "Instruction": *Connecticut River Review*, Summer 2018; "How to Keep the Devil Away": *Virginia Poetry Review*, Fall 2018; "What Do Men Want?" and "The Likelihood of Death": *The South Florida Poetry Journal*, Fall 2018; "During My Dark City Days," *West Texas Literary Review*, Winter 2019; "All the Ways I Have Sinned (The Lewis Place)," "Broken World," and "Beer Aisle Meditation," *Evening Street Review*, Fall 2019.

Part I: Memory's Blue Sedan

If harmony is
What you crave
Then get a tuba.

Burma-Shave

How a Single Word

Each childhood summer I found myself
back on the Southside of Virginia at my grandpa's
farm, tying up June bugs with twine,
watching them orbit the skinny planet that was myself, their emerald
bellies so beautiful in hot August suns, reflecting back
the mystery that is bug, light, and the buzzing symphony
of insect wings slicing the humid Southern air.

These days the soft Virginia dusks have sunken further
into memory, and the only way I can reach back is through
the steady beat of syllables that become words, that summon
scenes, that become the surprising cloth of whole worlds
spinning through another century, summoning my great-great grandpa

Sam, buried alive at the Battle of the Crater
in Petersburg, Virginia in 1864
as Lee and the Army of Northern Virginia struggled to survive
in the bloody days before Appomattox. His wife, Annie,
lost five infants after childbirth, so she never
named a daughter until she'd lived for a month.

Annie knew we have to be careful with names, how a single
word, *blue,* when added to another, *ridge,* becomes a whole
chain of mountains filled with oak, cedar, and tulip poplars
that spread their wings like angels in the greening spring.

Remembering a Palace of Shudders and Sighs

I have regular landscapes I dream so often
they become as real as the places they mirror in sleep,
those fields, those pastures, those barns,
that mean goat tied up in the back field behind the chicken coop.

There was a black and white goat, there were chickens,
there was an apple tree right next to the outhouse,
there was the smell of shit and lime, and across the path
there was a pig sty where the hogs wallowed
in mud and piss. It was all beautiful

in the way that real things bloom
in memory, become tangible again
as I reach back and touch Daisy,
the milk cow, who is brown and cranky
in the first light of a morning
long ago when I slept beneath handmade
quilts in a palace of shudders and sighs,
which was the wind, the trembling
pine, the floorboards and walls
in the house where all my dreaming began.

Last night I was there again, walking down
the narrow path defined by pickup and tractor
tires, wide enough for a boy and his yearning
to plunge into this brimming feast, to lose
himself in the woods, which were so alive
then, brimming with slow creeks and fast squirrels
and black bears that slumbered all winter
in caves carved out of the soft red clay.

Once, I got so lost in the forest, I could not find
my way out, and as the sun buried itself in the west,
the light shriveled and my heart pounded just
a little bit harder. I barely heard the blaring

horn that was my grandpa summoning
me back to the world of fresh biscuits
and fried chicken for dinner, to the soft Virginia voices
praising dead aunts and Jesus. Cursing tobacco
prices, the lame horse, the break in the fence
that let one of the cows escape, the *Richmond Times Dispatch*,
which we read days after it was published and days
before it would be taped over windows
that sometimes let in too much light.

Definitions

A good friend once told me to stop
writing about my grandpa.
She was tired of reading poems
set in the Southside of Virginia,

but here I am, sailing through a new century
still remembering the smell of tractor tires
and gasoline from the shed where the old
man worked on his John Deere
and cursed its rusty lack of motion,

which caused him to tether Billy Buck
to the tobacco sled filled with hopeful
green seedlings, and then he'd
follow the brown horse through
the cool spring fields, planting
row after row until the noontime dinner.

I've neglected to mention that
as my grandpa drove Billy Buck,
four black men walked along the sled,
rhythmically pulling out a seedling,
then pushing it into the red earth.

And later when we feasted on fried chicken,
mashed potatoes and snaps dripping
with hog grease, the black men ate
on the back porch as we gathered
in the kitchen. This was the world

in 1960. Poised before the fire
of great change, we dipped
homemade biscuits to our plates
and sopped up the tasty remnants
of our meal. I could hear the black

men laughing on the back porch.
And as I looked out an east window
the fields and forests shimmered
with the easy light of afternoon,
and it seemed for a moment
that the way things were right then,
was the way they would always be.

It Spoke Something Beautiful

My grandfather drank too much
and broke the kitchen chairs
on Saturday nights when we hid upstairs
in that dark bedroom I'm always returning to in dream
with its homemade quilts folded over two lumpy beds,
one for Mom and the other for the three of us kids
shivering beneath our heaven-bound breath.

All these years later, have I dreamed details into the setting,
added a mirror in the corner of the room, where right
now my mom is brushing her long black hair? Are the mud daubers real?
Spitting nests into the corners of high windows that
look out over the night fields
where the whippoorwills stir on the forest floor,
wailing into the night, truth telling
the sorrows of the world in every song?

Last Will and Testament: *Richmond, Virginia 1863*

My great-great-great grandfather, Peter Daniel
faced with the certainty of death, and the uncertainty of life,
left one-ninth of his estate to my great-great grandfather, Samuel Harrison
who was away fighting in the Civil War.

I'm looking at the names of Peter's slaves: Sam, Clara, John, Rhoda, Fannie
    and child, Sallie and two children, Letta and child.

However,

*We commissioners on examination find it impractical to divide said slaves in
nine equal lots and under said order and by consent of the parties have assigned
said slaves in five lots to wit…*

It doesn't say if Fannie kept her children,
or Sallie, or Letta,
and I suppose it says a lot
that the children are nameless
like the ten hogs
or the two barrels of nails
the old man left to Sam.

Through the glory of the Internet
I found out more about Peter Daniel,
how the Southside Virginia town where he lived in the 19th century
became Danieltown because of all the relatives who settled there.

After the war, the Daniels fell on hard times,
and when my uncle Jay visited the ancestral farm

in the late 1980s, it was owned by a black man
and the family cemetery had become a hog lot,
where sows and piglets rooted happily
among the fallen tombstones.

And can I tell you how many times I've thought
of children torn from their mothers,
how often I've dreamed of pigs and ghosts
and white bones shimmering in moonlight?

BIRTHRIGHT

When the sawmill opened at the edge
of my grandpa's farm, he told me
to watch out for the black men
who worked there, that they'd cut
the heart out of a little white boy like me.

I hated my grandfather's casual racism.
I hated the *whites only* signs that
were everywhere: the Esso station,
the soda fountain at Woolworths, how
my relatives spoke in hushed tones
about blacks, who it seemed to me,
were living identical impoverished lives
in a parallel universe with its own churches,
schools, neighborhoods—even the countryside
was the same: tobacco fields, pine forests, the muddy
creeks that cut red clay banks where sometimes
I'd find a quartz arrowhead or two, dislodged
by the slow current. These days

my grandparents and parents are dead, my aunts
and uncles winnowed down to a grey-haired few,
my many cousins scattered from Virginia to California
and I try, dear Lord, to forgive them all for their
narrow-mindedness, like the time my favorite uncle, Jay,
bragged about my great-great grandpa being lucky
to die in 1862 while the Confederacy still lived.

Uncle Jay also taught me how to play baseball
in a weedy field behind an outbuilding where
grandpa stored grain and flour. For hours on
weekend afternoons, he'd pitch to me
and I'd whack the ball into the woods
that began where the overgrown yard ended.
It was best to avoid the wasps and blacksnakes

when you parted bushes with your bare hands,
but that made the game more exciting, a little
danger at the edge of things like the uncertainty
that's always at the perimeter of our lives--

where right now I'm sitting in the lobby of a Florida hotel
watching Muhammad Ali's funeral parade in Louisville,
a flower-covered hearse glinting in the soft Kentucky sun.
The black cleaning lady vacuums red and blue carpets
which have yellow swirls that are somehow redemptive.
The young tattooed valet asks me if the sound is bothering
me as I type this in a sunlit corner, and I answer, "No, man.
I love that guy." Soon there's a dozen of us, black, white, Hispanic,
young and old, hotel workers, retired folks, a salesman or two,
all gathered to honor the Champ, who overcame all
in the name of a shining love, the same black man
my parents called "uppity" in the 1960s
when he was still Cassius Clay--draft dodger, soon-to-be Muslim--
who became a Savior delivering redemption in quick poems and fast fists
as he *floated like a butterfly and stung like a bee.*

The Map

Sometimes I feel like it's time to fold
up the map, with its circles for elevation,
greens for state and national parks, black
lines for those roads that go
to the places I'm most afraid of.
Somewhere in the dark, a farmhouse
flickers in memory like a ghost ship
sailing through the pastures and fields
of the mid-20th century. It was real
once, the house, the 1950s, the little boy
who searched for Jesus, the wild chickens
that wandered everywhere, constantly
underfoot, loud with their clucking
insanity. The world was solid then.
I dug holes in the sandy soil beneath
the dying oak tree. I shot Pepsi cans
with my uncle Jay's .22. I rode
tobacco sticks as if they were horses
until my thighs were chafed and the sun
began to hunker down somewhere west
of Victoria, Virginia. In memory the sunsets glow
and wither. In memory the stars come out
in skies so black the constellations blaze
with their clear meanings. In memory
an owl hoots; whippoorwills wail; a bobcat
cries from a place that is darker still.

All these things were real. Marked on a map
that shows me the way to get back to
Sundays filled with Bible verses, long dinners
at a table where my grandpa spoke grace
and all of us closed our eyes, picturing
beautiful things, almost hearing angels
as the old man wandered towards "Amen."

Now I'm wondering how much of my life
I've lived with closed eyes, searching for God,
listening for the whispered flight of doves,
praying in those quiet moments in between
for inspiration or health or a good tobacco crop,
or maybe a kiss from the golden-haired girl
who sat next to me in Sunday School
and made me so nervous I vibrated.

EVERY WHISPERED WORD
I believe in the flesh and the appetites... Walt Whitman

Once after my friend Rickey's mom
bought a new refrigerator, we took
the huge box to the side of a canyon
and rode in cardboard darkness
down an ice-planted hill. We pretended
we were in a homebound spaceship
as we rattled over the squishy slope, screaming out
to the inhabitants of Earth that we had returned.

For a long time I feared the return of Jesus
as laid out on the front page of my grandma's Bible,
His descent framed by purple clouds, lightning,
and the grinning faces of angels. Forgive me,

Father, but every whispered word in those days
was colored by fear: of punishment, of Hell,
of eternal separation from the ones we loved
like astronauts who had missed their target
and floated beyond death past
cold stars and uninhabited planets.

After hours of riding in the fridge box
we'd return to the clubhouse
in a corner of our duplex's garage
where we'd listen to early Beatles on the AM radio
and play War with cards featuring naked women.

I knew the cards and music were sinful,
as was the erection gathering beneath
my ice plant-stained jeans, but there was
such sweetness in the sound of the slapping cards,
in the harmonies of John and Paul, in the desire I felt
looking at a busty brunette who dominated the ace of clubs.
San Diego 1963

Imagining Sweden

When I was 10 years old, my mom
bought a cheap painting at Kmart that
showed a lake surrounded by snow-
capped mountains. I imagined it was
Sweden, and quite often in my childhood
I wanted to crawl over the couch and launch
myself into that alpine landscape, leaving
my loneliness behind and starting a new
life in a world filled with blonde, large-breasted
Nordic women. I knew they would love me,
pimples and all. I knew they would accept
all my sorrow and translate it into long
afternoons where one of the girls would
hold my hand as we stared into the lake,
until I'd forget I was merely a boy
who'd crawled into a picture--and everything
would become real: the soft hand of the girl,
the lake sparkling in all that afternoon light,
the wind a little too warm for the altitude,
but, hey, I'd never complain
as the sweet night darkened the water
and the stars scrawled their wistful calligraphy
in syllables of silver and white.

A Sky Language

What happens when your mom dies
and you have no one to tell
she was your best friend
when you were a kid, how your
dad was always off sailing with
the Seventh Fleet, and it was Mom
who walked with you that two miles
in 1965 to the Grossmont Shopping Center
to buy those baseball shoes with the rubber cleats?

She didn't know how to drive, so how
did she purchase Christmas presents
and later drag bikes and train sets up two flights
of stairs when she pretended to be Santa Claus?
In those holiday pictures, there is only the bounty
of gifts beneath the tree and my sister, brother and I,
playing in the morning light, my mother always behind
the camera, invisible. And yet,

I used to complain about dinners of beans
and collards, even the homemade cornbread. I never
understood that when you're poor, you're poor
and that's why you sleep in a dingy duplex and your
friends at school live on exalted La Mesa streets
with palm trees out front of big ranch style houses
with emerald yards and swimming pools out back.

Sometimes I'd get invited to pool parties
and wonder at the riches assembled
in those suburban palaces, and wonder
at the women who wore a lot of makeup
and nice clothes and who looked beautiful
in a Debbie Reynolds kind of way.

I grew to be ashamed of our lives, embarrassed
by my mother's Southern accent, which my friends
made fun of because it was so uncool.
My buddy Frank called me a hillbilly
and now, 50 years later, I celebrate
the soft ways my mother spoke, our humble
lives lived beneath the giant cross
that looked down upon us from atop Mount Helix.

I am left with memories
that rush toward me unbidden
as synapses crackle with old age
and quick meaning: my mom in a purple
sweater, in her late 20s, dark black hair
falling down her forehead. Even when I was
a kid, I was an insomniac, so for the first three
years of my life, she rocked me to sleep
and told me stories about the Three Bears
and Jesus—somehow fairy tales and the King James
Bible blended together in a kind of song
I fell asleep to. It's too late

to tell her how grateful I am now
for the Christmas presents, the school supplies,
the new clothes we wore each September—all the ways
she made love tangible, a sturdy thing
in a Southern California earthquake zone
where some days the world trembled
and the dishes my dad had brought back from Japan
rattled in the cupboard. We never used that pretty china,
nor did my sister play with the black-haired dolls
displayed above the saucers and bowls and cups
with their strange calligraphies in a light blue
that made me think of a sky language, of a way
of writing that was a beautiful way of knowing,
so foreign to me then but coming into focus

these days when sorrow speaks at dawn,
waking me to a new morning I remember
older mornings when I drank Tang and ate oatmeal
with lots of sugar before walking into golden
light that rode the soft shoulders of palm and eucalyptus.

Last night, two years after your death, Mom,

I dreamed you lived in a tiny apartment in Chicago
beneath some factory that churned out silverware,
and the whole time I visited, we could hear
the clanging of knives and forks being born upstairs.
You had me check out a leak in your bedroom
and indeed there was a little trickle
dripping down, probably ruining the drywall—
so, I said you'd better get a handyman right over
before the mold set in. In this dream, Mom, you'd
never fallen to dementia. You still walked with
a steady gait and when you spoke, every single
word made sense. When I awoke
the factory had vanished, so I made coffee
and whispered to myself the way we do
when dreams end too soon and the morning
burns outside the kitchen window, sets
this latest world on fire.

What the Man Dreams

The boy slept with his grandmother until he was 10
in a world where woods crept up to the edges of the yard,
to the margins of each field, to the gravel-covered road that
led to a wider dirt road, which finally reached
asphalt some 20 miles later. The boy in old age

will dream of the road, the farmhouse, his grandparents,
the hen house, the apple tree with its bitter Winesaps;
he will dream of the bright stars of those days before light pollution,
the way the night sky seemed to spring from his grandmother's
fingertips as she whispered names toward the constellations,
giving meaning to hunters and swans. When it was time

for sleep, the boy would crawl beneath homemade
quilts and his grandmother would read a poem or two
about white men and cavalry charges, or nature of tooth
and claw, or a waterfall's miracle of time suspended, motion
and stasis, forever. And at last the boy prayed,
asked God to bless every relative, then every human on earth,
and at last the animals, until the boy had honored a whole
world of creatures in the beautiful repetition of *God bless*.

These days the boy thinks back to the magic of his grandmother,
the unpolluted night sky filled with the design of a Creator
who spoke the universe into being, everything from stars
and planets to Billy Buck, the plow horse who sweated
through each planting season, pulling a sled of tobacco leaves.

The man wonders when exactly he stopped praying before sleep,
and grew world-weary and unsure. So he conjures
his grandmother, the quilted bed, the lilac scent of her skin,
the flowered gown she slept in, night after night,
the way she held him until he fell asleep; and it was a gentle fall,
soft and airy, filled with echoes of *God bless, God bless, God bless,*

until there was no world, no God, no grandmother, until he dreamed
of the woods he'd run through all summer long, the neighbor's black
bull with the red halter around its neck, the big-toothed pike in a pond
just past the clearing at the edge of loblolly pine,
the singing of whippoorwills at dusk.

Coronado

I wake often from dreams of my dead parents,
having just visited childhood houses, abandoned parks,

a sunlit beach in Coronado
where my father and I waded out into the green waves,
as he held me up over the white curl, kept me above
the roar that would become surf crashing to the wet sand
that gave a little, revealed perfect sand dollars. Again, last night,
my father's hands around my waist, the California sun slipping
from afternoon into evening, shadows lengthening on the beach:
boy and man, son and father in a temporary embrace
of sun and sea, the cold, warm, desperate surge
of things above and things below, of flesh, spirit,
and voices screaming, even now, with fear and delight.

Why My Porn Name is Gus Lineberry

In 1967 when I was 12, my parents rented a cramped three-bedroom house on Lineberry Road in Virginia Beach. Shortly after we moved in, I helped my mom open the little plywood door that led to the attic, and I'm not making this up: an unsealed envelope fell out and showered us with black and white pictures of a grown woman, naked from the waist up, smiling back at the camera, her chubby face, short hair, and big boobs framed then and forever in my memory, even though my mom quickly gathered up the photos and threw them in the trash. All night long, I schemed sneaking into the kitchen and retrieving those pictures, which I finally did, only to find them cut into tiny pieces that held no naked meaning, no nipples, no pale skin, no freckles cascading down from her shoulders like the uneven dots for cities along highways that lead to a foreign land's lush interior, a place where papayas and star fruit grow in a confusion of fruit and flowers affirming how the flesh will somehow endure in quiet places near remote villages that sprawl toward a single smoking volcano.

All the Ways I Have Sinned

In those days we'd gather
on Sunday afternoons after church
for big meals in my grandma's kitchen.
The world sparkled beyond every window
in its hymn of pine and sunlit pasture
as I listened to my grandpa offering grace
during a time when being grateful seemed less
like a chore and more just a way of being in that world
where *Jesus* sprang softly from the lips
of everyone I loved. After dinner, the afternoon

stretched out with its Wiffle ball games in the backyard,
and I'd sprint across the soft grass, hear the commotion
from the driveway next to the smokehouse
where my grandpa and uncles drank
bourbon hidden in paper bags,
their faces blushing with secret pleasure that
made them laugh louder than the whining engine
they pretended to be working on, half-
heartedly fiddling with a carburetor flap,
reconnecting a spark plug wire to the gapped
Champion that would bring fire to the pistons'
galloping in the afternoon sun. The women

stayed inside and chronicled the illnesses of relatives
in hollows down dirt roads that led to dark leafy
places where the nights were as quiet as death.
There was Aunt Lorraine who had "the sugar diabetes"
slowly taking the toes on her right foot,
and there was Uncle Harry, confined to bed
in the last years of lung cancer brought on
by the bull's-eyed packs of Lucky Strikes.

It's taken me this long to remember that the farm
was called the Lewis Place, because my grandparents

rented it from a man called Lewis, whom I never met,
but I can see that house so clearly now, with its big
front porch, and the yard with the walnut tree
that ended at the edge of the soybean fields, which ran
down to the single-lane road, beyond which
shimmered a cattail-fringed pond filled with large-
mouth bass, bream, and water moccasins
that swam powerfully through the shallows,
reminding all of us that terrible things lurked
just beneath the surface of our world, waiting for us
to fall away from the living god, luring
us toward sin. I do not

have words for all the ways I have sinned
since those childhood days on the Lewis farm
but I do have memories of bars in a great city
where I drank beauty and sorrow away, that Janus-
faced truth about our lives, how what we think we love
are always the things we are most afraid of losing, but we
only watch silently as lovers walk out the front door, or
drink again after a few days of stormy abstinence, or
we simply give up to the cold light that is the latest morning
on the highway sprawling west toward the rest of our lives.

All the Sorrow

I took a walk earlier this afternoon
and thought about my grandfather,
how in his latter days, he retreated to his bed
and took solace in the fire of Jim Beam. I judged
him then: old alcoholic, bad father, mean husband;
what did I know about raising tobacco
and a brood of twelve children, six boys and six girls,
all with hungry mouths to feed? I remember most
clearly the *Groucho Marx Show* on a black and white Philco,
both of us mesmerized and laughing in the early evening,
when outside dusk was building over the woods
as the whippoorwills began to cry, and all the sorrow
of the world was spreading through a million leaves.

I'd understand my grandfather many years later,
when I drank my own life away in Chicago,
spent most of my time drinking at home
or sometimes at ball games or taverns
or restaurants or bowling alleys or even at
the Suds N Brew on Southport, where I'd
get drunk at the bar while my clothes
were spinning in machines I'd loaded with quarters.

I still remember the taste of cold drafts at the tavern,
the sounds of the jukebox, the way smoke rose
in grey swirls—and it was almost like we were all on fire,
sacred creatures with thick tongues speaking a kind of scripture
that prophesied the fall of man, as Joe, the Polish bartender,
refilled our glasses, as afternoon bled into evening,
beneath stars made invisible by city lights.

All the Troubles

Dreaming Chicago's long retreat into memory
when 20 below mornings
tattooed skin like a crude Canadian awl.
Pages and pages of scenes from this life
and another one I whispered on dark corners
like North and Clybourn, or Randolph and Halsted
or anywhere else a tavern burned
through the haze of city life
and offered its sweet forgetfulness
of booze and more booze, of sermons
in a bottle, sermons in a keg,
and resurrection into an afterlife
where Mabel brings the Black Label
and all that is holy is spiked with alcohol.

These days verses bleed into each other
until the gospel sings of blood and bird,
of industrial furnaces and wings of night,
a bible of the dying world where past and present
shape smoke and motion into a ledger of loss, the words
tumbling down in past storms and tribulations, the inky
truth writ here at last: indeed, *the wages*
of sin is death as the sign outside a storefront
church blared into the darkness of Lake Street,
only to meet the pink glare of the TNT Lounge
advertising the best chicken wings in town.
Wages is a singular way of earning death,
a working man's reward for hours behind the wheel,
behind the locomotive, behind the counter, behind the vein
of coal that is slowly burning its way to diamond, behind
the eight ball on the pool table at the Zebra Lounge
sequestered in the cottony dark of Rush Street, Chicago, 1978.
I swim back in time, dreaming of bars and prostitutes,
of being so drunk the world didn't hurt anymore, that singular
release from all the troubles daylight would bring.

The label on a bottle of Jim Beam, speaking
of proof and age, good things in bourbon,
indeterminate things in men who are always changing,
reassembling in lies spoken each morning that eventually
add up to years of drinking, a long road to a dead end
at the end of a small town in western Wisconsin
where on Friday nights, the locals gather for a fish fry.

1968

Sometimes before sleep when the moon
has ceased its yellow howling
and the stars burst like silver
berries into the palm of the sky's hand,
I can hear the emptiness
of a thousand prairies where the struggling
rivers of summer whisper past the cottonwood
trees. Where are the bison? Where are the horse
people who camped in the foothills of the Bighorn
Mountains and screamed the morning light
in syllables of blood and sweat until the words
of whole nations thundered across the high
grasses of now dead places? Where is the grace
in a single minute out of the wind, one minute
when the humming buzz of invisible things
is forgotten and at last the light is heard,
when the ears turn away from music
and listen to the pink contrails of sunrise?

But I have tinnitus, so the wind never stops
and the bison thunder all night. I must play
games to trick myself into silence, which comes
at the beginning of a dream
where a window opens to a world I had not expected
to be in the living color of late 1960s TV sets:

My lover's face is slightly green. I adjust the tint
but can't get it right. Behind her B-52s bomb
green rice paddies that stretch from jagged
mountains to a surging sea. Everywhere the fire
burns in the old vacuum tubes that
need to be replaced by repairmen every month or so,
and for a while the TV is silent
as we look around for meaning
in ourselves but we've lost that language,

so we go to bed early and dream of napalm,
of a time when Buddhist priests
burned themselves in protest,
their yellow-robed bodies perfectly still
until they were completely smoke. The dark
shadows they left behind were celebrated
by children who knew the power of immolation,
the way the sacred lives on the very tip
of each flaming tongue.

The Past

Ever since both my parents died within a week of each other
last July, I've been trying to write my way out of grief, into
the kinds of meaning that flash like little brown wrens
in the morning garden, healing intuitions, tiny recognitions
that come only with a winged beat. Of course, it rarely
happens, those moments where the secret arrives
with the very next line, or the balm for aching pain
flowers within an earthly heart like sunlight warming
a winter field. Or is it a pasture where a cow munches
on wild onions, which will ruin next morning's milk,
or is it the henhouse where the chickens wander
happily, not knowing that by afternoon two of them
will have their necks wrung, and then they will be sacrificed
and plucked, delivered with the dumplings and fresh
carrots that are so orange they might be part of a summer
sunset, a fading sky of vegetables, the last colors purple
like the bitter turnips my dad said you could never squeeze
blood from. My parents did their best

with little, stretched dollars until
George Washington grimaced. They shopped at
the Navy Exchange and thrift stores galore, bought
day-old bread and doughnuts at the Dolly Madison outlet
where aging baked goods had been sent to die.

When you're a kid, you just don't get that you're poor,
can't understand why all your friends have new bikes
and yours is the clunker with the rusty chain.

In 1968 we moved to Daytona Beach and lived in a house
with a big live oak out back where sometimes my dad
would hit me grounders until it got too dark to see
except for the vague shapes of things disappearing: the baseball,
my dad with that peculiar way he held the bat, his arms crossed
over each other as he whacked the last one-hopper

towards me in the strange twilight of those days
with dusk bringing dinner and long nights in front of the TV
watching sitcoms until bedtime when
I retreated to my lower bunk
and worried about my little brother
falling on me. For some reason,

it seems important to note that in the late 1960s
Mom started buying Roman Meal instead of white bread, an early nod
toward better nutrition, so she'd pile on the bologna and American
cheese, slather it all with mayo, and send us off with our brown bags
into the Florida morning, little centurions marching toward our battles
with math and the mean kids in gym class who'd knock us down
when our backs were turned. I learned early

on, it did no good to complain about bullies or bologna, that life
was full of cheap lunch meat and bruises. The best I could hope
for was to endure it all until I could get home and read
and escape to a stranger, more beautiful world. Reading this far,

it's probably hard to see how much I loved my parents,
how from time to time, I knew how much they sacrificed so I could get
that spacer from the dentist, or have enough
money to pay for Little League.
What did I know, what did I know of a world that was hard and tilted
against the poor, who will always be with us, scraping together enough
money for school clothes and those visits to the doctor with ice cold hands.

One World at a Time

Memory rumbles like an old sedan
rolling over the gravel driveway
that leads to a farmhouse
I dreamed last night in the haze
of sleep, the blurry pages turning,
bright windows opening to fields
and pastures where daylight
clings to the horizon, forging a new
world that is more real than the home
movie showing all the aunts
and uncles gathered on a Sunday afternoon
to laugh at the children playing in a backyard
so green in memory, it burns my eyes.
I can't stop the camera's revelations, how once
the world was new and vivid, how once
my heart opened to the sky and stayed
past dusk, at last drinking in the white
light of distant stars, the half-night
of moon and fireflies in the shade
of a world, turning, even then
toward sleep, toward the lights going out
one by one in farmhouses outside of towns
small enough to need only one drug
store and one bar. Towns, not cities, populations
measured in a few thousand, not millions, and best
of all the stars zoomed down and whispered bright
nothings until the children fell asleep. I fell

asleep beneath country stars and woke up
to sunny windows in an old house where daddy-longlegs
crept up high windows towards corners where the silken
webs gleamed like a tiny universe, which in a way they were,
strands afire like streams of matter, defining one space
among many in those places where wall and ceiling met,
interstices I witnessed in the way a small god might assemble

meaning, one web, one world at a time until there were
many worlds burning in that old house. And now I hear
Grandma whispering, *If you kill a daddy longlegs, all your
cows will die.* And even in this future without cattle,
I love hearing the old woman's voice.

The Light of Other Days

Went out back, shoveled some black
soil around my cherry tomato plants
and weeded everywhere with my hoe.
Turkey vultures circled overhead on lazy thermals
across a blue January sky, background for bird shows,
for waving branches of areca, even for the frayed
uneven growth at the top of a huge slash pine,
so tall, each time I gaze into the mystery
of its tangled branches, I think
of childhood, of pine trees in Virginia
dimming in a Southern sun as it sank low
into the western edge of my entire world,
where the Nottoway River separated
one farm from another as it thrummed south
toward Emporia, flooding low pastures, turning black loam
into blacker mud. Sometimes when I consider
the light of other days, it's almost like time (which itself holds memory)
is a river or creek, where we paddle with the current
and find ourselves always downstream,
our lived lives behind us, ghosts disappearing into the shadows
of black alder, sweetgum and Carolina willow.

At Last, Heaven

I am so much like the darkness
I spoke last night. There were
stars burning my tongue, and
I could almost touch the hems
of clouds that lingered at the
river's edge. You know that
river, so wide and so sluggish
you think it carries your entire
life and the lives and dreams
of everyone you've ever known.
I spoke darkness and water,
I spoke fishes darting in the
shallows amid the reeds
that sang in the wind. Yes,
there was music in my sleep
beyond the syllables of my
singed tongue, beyond anything
I might have previously known
in my waking life. Words, fish,
darkness, rivers, dreams, clouds
swimming in the liquid deep,
looking for sentences to shape
them, looking for meaning
in the rushing syntax of current
and night. The water was muddy
and warm. Small towns sparkled
from the river banks, which themselves
climbed away toward pastures and fields
where families slept in that moonlit sea
and dreamed constellations singing down,
and dreamed angels singing down, until
the whole night became a chorus
that I was speaking into, one voice

amid the dreaming many, one spirit
among the multitudes who turn in sleep
to seek our god. In daylight we live

the illusion of our separate lives,
venture forth to work the fields,
or tend to machines in the great
factories, or we march to gleaming
towers in humming cities where each
day we are wounded in ways
we could not have imagined in our dreams
the night before when our voices were lost in the river
until every part of us was lost in the river,
until all that remained was the hymn of night
and water, until our spirits danced like fireflies,
until the lights of our insect bellies diminished,
until, until, I became all of you and all of you
became me, until all of our voices bled into
the very song the night had been singing.

Memory's Blue Sedan

Because the storm last night woke me up
to that dark and bright world of rain
and lightning, because the dog snored
softly at my feet, because dark hair
traced the outline of your face on the pillow,
because the clock radio flashed
numbers I could not quite make out,
because sleep is the vehicle for memory
and its blue sedan swerved around
curves where Burma-Shave signs warned
of one-eyed cars and twinkling stars,
because I was still riding in the blue
sedan when I woke up—

I pushed my right leg toward
the brake pedal and panicked
when there wasn't one, tried hard to stop
the momentum of bed-sedan, until
I finally fell into this world, *this world*
where I got up and walked the dog down
a quiet suburban street and looked up
to see a complete rainbow in the western
sky, rising over the Gulf, while in the east,
dawn brought meaning to the slash pine,
palms, the crimson bougainvillea and
the yellow blossoms of Bahama cassia.
Look at how the gaining light flames
the red petals of firebush, which already
sing with bees and zebra longwing butterflies!

It would be nice to end here with the images
of flowers and butterflies, believing the present
has finally overcome the past, but I still live
in a world of nocturnal car rides with ghosts
who reach under the front seat

for Jim Beam in a brown bag, which
they raise to their lips like a sacrament.
And how their Adam's apples wiggle
as they take the fire into their bodies,
as I wonder about the strange notion
of all of us carrying original sin in our throats,
a hard, seeded bulb that bears stunning fruit:
centuries of guilt from the memory of a garden.

Until I was a Direction

Poems used to make me shiver
because I ate them like the red heart
of a sweet watermelon, cooled by the night that
is now fading into memory of fields and pastures
where the child wandered with his eyes open
to the dreams of honeysuckle and the way
each field ended at the edge of a forest
where all the answers whispered from
the trees. I ran toward that place
I prayed would save me. For years,

I've tried to describe the way the woods
called to me, how I wanted to answer
by losing myself in shadows forever, by walking
west until I was a direction myself, a cardinal point
on a compass, a destination so remote when it snows
there is no one to shovel, no plows scrape the icy
meaning away, and for miles the silence falls
into more silence. I'd learn to speak a language
of the spirit, that quiet without syllables, without
the stutter of machines or even pretty wind chimes
softening the city air like bells in a country church
calling out to lost souls on Sunday mornings.

Part II: Confluence

Woe to all
Sinners who
This way pass.

Burma-Shave

Confluence

Woke up this morning with a headache
after dreaming of the Little Bighorn
and dead bluecoats floating above
a sea of brown creosote. Goodbye,
George Armstrong Custer, I'll see
you and your arrow-pierced penis
in another dream, but for now I've
awakened in Florida, the flowered
land, and I have a headache. Maybe
it was my own eardrums the Sioux
women pierced with awls last night
so I might truly listen in
the world that comes next?

But right now, I hear only the hum
of the refrigerator in the kitchen
and the occasional crackle of the ice
maker as it summons its own glacier.
I don't see Indians riding beneath
a blue Montana sky. I don't hear
the swoosh of arrows, the din of
bullets and hooves. Sometimes
I sit amazed at the confluence
of history and the perpetual present,
how everything that was and everything
that is become all that will be. Yesterday,
my grandmother washed my hair
in water she'd collected from rain barrels
that had trapped a summer downpour.
Yesterday, I wondered at the grace
of a dragonfly hovering over
brown lake grasses. Yesterday,
I looked out a farmhouse window
and saw an entire green world rushing
to the blue horizon. Yesterday,

lightning bugs danced at the edges
of fields imprisoned by rusted barbed wire.
Yesterday, I sang hymns at St. Mark's
each Sunday and tried to believe
in an almighty God. Yesterday
the grasses stirred on forgotten
Montana hills, each bright leaf a soldier,
each green blade a shimmering Christ.

CHILD OF THE CORN!

I woke up this morning
with these words rattling in my head:
The aliens have installed a brain in the refrigerator.
And I thought: an alien brain? Is the fridge sentient?
Should I say "hello" to it this morning when I reach for the milk?
What would my wife think if she walked into the kitchen and saw
me having a conversation with the refrigerator?
Where would the aliens have installed the brain, anyway?
In the back with the compressor?
So many questions for a single, humming appliance.

I think sometimes those words we wake up with
are dreams trying to break through
and speak the mystery. Once I woke
up saying "Kansas." I suppose
that's more interesting than *refrigerator*;
after all, Kansas brings wheat fields
and the ghosts of dead Sioux gathering
amid the cottonwood trees where they
still pray for our deaths. The refrigerator
is merely a cold repository for the dead
flesh of animals, the pale skins of factory-
farmed vegetables, Monsanto legacies
in the too-green lettuce, the tasteless
beets and non-spicy radishes. If, however, there

really was an alien brain in the refrigerator,
and that refrigerator was in Wichita, maybe
it could think really hard about all that's happened
these last 12,000 years since the Neolithic, and maybe
the alien brain could save Kansas from corporate
farming and Christian fundamentalists?

You are what you eat.
So I am the sum of genetically altered corn,
cows and chickens raised on corn,
even my ice cream sweetened with corn
syrup. On a cellular level, I am one
with the corn. I am a child of the corn
and perhaps I will wander this earth
with all you other children of the corn
and modern life will come to resemble a corny sci-fi
B-movie where we fervently worship
a crucified corn god.

Alien brains, refrigerators, corn,
corporate farming, Christianity, Kansas.
I sit here with my coffee and consider
the basic corniness of my disposition,
how, perhaps, even the great Whitman
had it wrong: we do not come back
as the waving grasses; instead, we
are resurrected in the very stalks of corn,
and why is it that in some far off corner
of this poem, I see the smoke of the combine,
hear the thrashing of sharp blades,
hear the alien sound of a coming apocalypse?

I'D RATHER BE A COWBOY

In my composition class on Monday
I'm asked if the world will end on April 23rd
as predicted by a Christian cult.

I wanted them to ask me about the difference
between an independent and dependent clause.

I asked another student to give me an example of a gerund.

He told me he'd rather identify a different part of speech.

I told him I'd rather be a cowboy.

Because, if I were a cowboy, I could ride my horse across
the Great Plains, past the remnants
of Crow encampments, past the chattering
prairie dog towns, up and down a thousand hills
until I reached the shadow of the snowy Big Horns.
Yes, I'd much rather be a cowboy
in Wyoming, where geologic
time has stiffened the landscapes
into a ragged beauty of buttes and crevasses
that seems permanent, though we know
it is not. For a moment, however,
on my horse riding beneath the unending
sky, I could pretend that I was immortal,
that the mountains at the edge of this world
are sentinels praising more
mountains that linger beyond their jagged
summits. But beyond those mountains

is merely Idaho. Two hundred years ago
the Crow thought that beyond the mountains
lived another entire world that we entered
through smoking holes in the sky. Another

world with its own mountains, its own bison,
its own flurry of storms in April.
I imagine Indian paintbrush
blooming in Crow heaven. I imagine a prairie
storm that comes on so quickly the creosote
barely has time to lie down before the rain.

After reading Phil Levine,

I imagine a farmer who lives outside of Ames, Iowa, and yes, he takes a break from harvesting row after row of brown-tasseled corn, and yes, he is reading poems and considering what *work really is*, and yes, he left the combine running, and yes, a spark from the hot diesel leaps up to the dry stalks, and yes, a fire erupts amid the long avenues of browning green, and yes, within minutes the combine blows up, sending black smoke toward the blue late summer sky, and yes, the farmer looks up from the poem and yes, he's running toward the fire, waving his arms, singeing his yellow checkered shirt, which is flannel, which is too hot for an August day like this one when the flames are spreading northwest with the hot wind, and yes, the deer scatter, and yes, the wild turkeys have taken flight from those marginal woods that separate one burning field from another field that will soon be burning, until all of northern Iowa is a raging inferno, visible to the astronauts circling in the International Space Station, and yes, from space it looks like an apocalypse, but, no, from space they can't see that solitary farmer, who so much earlier in this poem set the world on fire through the negligence of reading a different poem, one that has been reduced to ashes that blow and scatter across field and prairie, but later after the fire has finally burned itself out, after the farmer and his family are given blankets and iced tea by the local Red Cross, after the farmer stops mourning all that he has lost, he begins to be grateful for all that was saved: his wife; his two red-headed daughters; his border collie, Vince; wedding album pictures that show them 30 years ago when the whole world was hope and the promise of fertile fields, and yes, he is grateful for all these things, and yes, even though it distracted him at the moment he should have heeded the early flames, and yes, he should have looked up from that excellent poem, but despite all of this, he finds himself still grateful for that dreamy, buttermilk moon.

Here's a Leap

Often in dreams I return to the tobacco curing barn,
that magical place where my grandpa
and uncles hung leaf-heavy sticks to the rafters
high above a kerosene heater on a dirt floor

that would never see sunlight. But, mostly,
there was the sweet scent of those leaves turning
from green to yellow, from plant to magic potion.
I can still smell the curing tobacco

years after cigarettes were vilified
until these days when you can't smoke most places
and the real money's made shipping cancer sticks
to China, where the ghosts of 9th-century poets

still wander smoky landscapes, admiring the solitary
heron hunting near the morning river, breathing
in the cool air that rolls in from the green fields
stretching all the way to the mountains. They knew

the secret: empty your mind so completely, you let the smoke
of landscapes fill your no longer thinking self, until
you are only the gentle rush of the river, the soft splash
of wading birds, the hum of the living world.

I believe in compassion

floating everyone's boat
like the paper ones released by lovers into tiny rivers,
little crinkled hopes, white as the dress of a shy village girl,
her red lips the cherry blossoms you've long desired. But she's
the river merchant's young wife, so be careful.
He may yet return from that place where he trades
fungi for watercolors, mushrooms for the inevitable
paintings of birds and the dead. Or he might not return,
or you yourself might assume a woman's identity,
embody sorrowful yearning and feel your heart
skip beats when you see hooded men in the distance,
stirring up dust, their horses mightier than the pen
with which you write these poems, these little
vessels filled with all the moonlight
you captured in your hands last night
when you raced across a field
of mustard flowers toward the sea.

These days the cold
comes slowly to your mountains
and you love the quiet mornings best
when you hear only the crackling frost
as a world awakens to the slow dream of winter.
What will you have for breakfast?
Perhaps some rice seasoned with sorrow
or stringy pieces of the blessed chicken
whose neck you wrung
yesterday in the silent afternoon
when grey clouds gathered above the mountains
whose summits were swirling
with the ghost breaths of everyone you have ever loved.

Out of the Midst of the Fire

And I looked, and, behold, a whirlwind came out of the north, a great cloud, and a fire infolding itself, and a brightness was about it, and out of the midst thereof as the colour of amber, out of the midst of the fire. Ezekiel 1:3

Here I am sitting at my desk
on a sunny Saturday with a brain buzzing
on caffeine and a fervent desire to go back to bed.
A tiny voice whispers, *but what if you missed
out on writing that poem you've been waiting
for your entire life* about
collecting blackberries in a dented steel pot,
late summer on the Southside of Virginia,
hands bleeding from the brambles,
head spinning from the sugar
of the potent, ripe berries?

My entire life has been a hunt
for the quick fix, whether it was sugar
in my childhood, or drugs and booze
when I became a broken adult.
So little to say, and so much time
to say how the insults of the years
added up to varicose veins, arthritic knees,
and those weird floaters that swim
across my eyes like water bugs
dancing across the surface of a pond
in 1960, when I was a boy fishing
for sweet yellow-bellied bream
down the hill from a road
that wound through the pine
forests during a time of great sorrow
in my own little life.

Lately, I've been considering Ezekiel's
scary encounter with four-faced
twirling creatures of fire
and I wonder about the power of imagination
to remake the world into angels and demons
like my sweet grandmother and alcoholic grandfather,
the yin and yang
of a world where I was slowly
becoming myself, a creature with only
one face, with no wings and no luminosity,
who never lifted off the earth
in a wheel of burning feathers.

My Heart

Those railroad tracks outside of Omaha where the boxcars are shunted.
Those hobo ghosts who sleep in boxcars and sometimes sing Woody Guthrie songs around an imaginary campfire.
Those yellow-orange flames, the soot and cinders, the tender grave of coals.
The chuck-will's-widow with a broken wing.
Those skies the bird would have flown into, the possible nights, the days that might have been.
Those liquid centuries of sky filled with cumuli, nimbi, scud, and sometimes a moon or a twinkling planet or two.
Those astronomers who gaze into the Cosmos and feel famished but not diminished.
Those dogs that sleep quietly at the feet of astronomers and dream of rivers gleaming beneath starlit nights.
The rivers themselves, trusty redeemers of geologic time, mountain-born, ocean-bound.
The river valleys filled with black cottonwoods.
The cottonwoods wild with green wind.
The cattails on the river banks.
The tadpoles lingering amid the cattails.
The bream that might have been.
The train whistle in the distance, shrinking miles and memory.
The locomotive pounding, the boxcars filled with freight for dusty western towns.
The hobo ghosts, still playing guitars and chewing Red Man.
The brown spittle, the juice that's always good for snakebite.
The snake that bites, the diamondback gleaming in a dusk pine barren.
The serpent, an apple, a garden, a tenderness, a betrayal, a man, a woman, a serpent.
A train whistle at a railroad crossing, midnight, 20 miles from the closest town.

55

The closest town, population 500, not including transients who wait in dark yards for night bound trains, always aiming west.
A tenderness of Western gardens, strawberries in Watsonville, wild peaches in lost canyons,
Navajo ghosts painting with desert sand.
A serpentine track past white summits, the cold stars leaning down, whispering.
The wind.
The grave of coals, the fading embers, the sacred text drawn by fire.
The locomotive.
The horse people who feared the trains.
The bison.
The Continental Divide where meaning falls one way and another at the same time, where rivers aim east or west, where trails die out in canyons, where the wind is a long hiss.
Histories of St. Louis, the Falls of the Missouri, and Seaside, Oregon.
A whole historic expedition drunk on whiskey and exploration.
Skinny winter deer.
The unlucky dogs roasted over a fire by Lewis and Clark.
The salmon Lewis and Clark ignored.
Christ, the beautiful salmon!

My First Marriage Compared to the Lewis and Clark Expedition

Our love was in the flesh once, and we drove
this country in a 1971 Impala,
its badly aimed headlights drifting from asphalt
to the periphery's bullet-riddled
signs that exaggerated population.
On broken shocks, we bounced into Iowa, found
towns shadowed by Mississippi cliffs, Davenport,
Bettendorf with fading Victorian houses
patrolled by mean dogs in overgrown yards
rising high above the muddy river.
To the west the sunset was dust and blood
filling the horizon's curve as the early
stars broke through the Midwestern sky.

That first night we huddled in a musty motel
bed, chased a bottle of Bushmills down
past its label bringing late fire to our bellies,
drowsy heat in our brains, with the TV late
into test patterns as the night trucks rumbled by,
shaking the plywood walls and the picture
of Jesus looking down from over our king-size bed.

My travel-stained journal
traced our trip like Lewis and Clark's,
noting the Corps of Discovery
went north and west, while my wife and I journeyed
in a drunken circle beginning and ending in Chicago.
A common thread can be seen
running through both expeditions:
bad things happened when the whiskey ran out.

One hundred days of rain and depression
for Meriwether Lewis, he of the ironic
first name. Huddled on the Oregon coast,
feasting on dogs and the skinny, starving deer

whose eyes burned darkly in the grey-
shrouded landscape of rain and more rain,
Lewis stopped writing, thought back to St. Louis
and the trip's fine beginning aboard boats
loaded with muskets, pretty beads for Indian trade,
and most important, barrel after barrel of whiskey.

Our money and liquor ran low in Kentucky,
after we twisted south through Illinois,
across the state line at Paducah,
then fled east to Lexington where pretty brown
horses loped behind miles of perfect white fences.
Our last 10 dollar bill bought a bottle
of Brass Monkey, a six-pack of Falls City
beer, and two large cups filled with ice
that glittered in the windshield's captured sun.
We drank along the green back roads
leading to towns like Paris and Versailles
where the locals drawled
in a language far removed from French.
We French-kissed through a drunken haze,
chased the last of the hard stuff with warm beer
until a full Kentucky moon rose from a wooded hill
somewhere way east of Frankfurt.

The next day, hung-over and dull-eyed
from sleeping in the Impala (whose sprinting
antelope had long sprung, left an emptiness over the hood),
we toured the Shaker town at Pleasant Hill
overlooking the Kentucky River, and wondered
about the perfect furniture within
the perfect houses occupied by chaste ghosts.

They died content within their whirling
trances, sober to the light of their last day.

We boarded the Impala, darkened Interstate 64
north toward the Indiana line.

And across the Ohio,
late-afternoon hills pretended
to be mountains.

Part III: Modern Life

In this world of toil and sin
Your head grows bald
But not your chin

Burma-Shave

At a Supermarket in South Florida,

Whitman gazes at me through the eyes
of an old woman who wants
that last helping of pineapple
the nice Publix lady is handing out.
Even though I know the yellow flesh
is good for my inflamed prostate
I move on to other matters
of fruit and vegetables. Kale
for example, full of iron and vitamins,
a deep cosmic green that makes me dream
of acres and acres of tobacco in a Virginia sun.
It's odd that the prettiest leaves were poison.

There's the old woman again, standing in front
of the narrow display of free-range chicken,
each package with a website that will take
me to the farm where the chicken was raised
by a nice family. If I imagine deeply
enough, I can travel to that farm,
inhale the deep calm of those green pastures
where it feels like a man can settle down,
raise his own family with his own chickens,
maybe even have a cow or two for fresh milk.

And if I imagine even deeper I can travel into
the past of that family, see a grandpa
tilling a field of 19th-century radishes. Grandma
sits in the kitchen reading an *Old Farmer's Almanac*,
which says the coming winter will be the worst
in 50 years, how it would be best to harvest and can
all the blackberries and cucumbers so that January
might still be filled with sweetness and crisp
pickles on the white bread sandwiches that speak
of a time when plain was fine. That's quite a website,

so I'd better be sure not to linger too long in its familiar
foreign lands, and be sure not to covet the farmer's
daughter whose hair is flaxen and whose breasts
rise and fall beneath her lilac blouse, which promises
even more flowers and a feast of white skin and nipples
so dark, I can't help but gasp when I touch them,
which is a mistake I can't come back from, and now
I live on the farm in the website and clean the chicken
coop each morning before gathering eggs for my new
wife to scramble into breakfast. I can't wait
to eat them along with the hot buttered biscuits
buried in fresh blackberry preserves.

When the Cashier at the Grocery Asks Me

If I've found everything OK, I make
a joke about not being able to locate
the ground reindeer horn I need
for this afternoon's séance. She doesn't
laugh, blips my blueberries, apples,
peanut butter, soy milk, and coffee
into more dollars than I'd expected.
I want to tell her, besides the reindeer horn,

I couldn't find the joy I felt as a child
every time I jumped into a summer lake,
or the happiness I felt simply being
in my body as I ran across California
yards that glow greener in memory.
I want to tell her, I'd like to find
that place, where in 1962, I realized
depression was my best friend, how
I could give myself up to sadness
and relax into its slow music, as I hid
from my mother, who'd want me
to cut the grass or wash dishes
when I preferred being alone,
feeding my hungry sorrows
until dusk, when I'd sneak into
my room and pray, *God
bless Mom, Dad, Grandma, Grandpa
and everyone else in the world. Please,
Lord, please, feed the starving children in India,
make sure the Russians don't kill us, and is it possible
Linda might dance with me this weekend?*

Hairdresser of the Dead

The woman who washes my wife's hair
tells her she's a mortician's assistant,
and spends her weekdays
preparing the dead. She's only
working part time at the beauty shop
because business is slow these days,
the only people dying are *old people
and Mexicans*, she says. *What's really
weird is that when you wash a dead
person's hair, their ears move.* Business
is also bad because more people are
choosing cremation, picking fire over
slow disintegration, a quick burst
over entropy. *The Mexican
dead are beautiful*, she says.
*They're always dressed in white,
and the children look so lifelike,
I expect them to rise from the casket.*

Once though, she accidentally pulled
off the scalp of a 5-year-old girl
but managed to fix it before the viewing.
It's so important to honor the dead
she tells my wife. I hear this story

hours later and imagine the beautiful Mexicans,
clad in the purest white, dancing in Paradise.
I imagine the dead waking in their radiant clothes,
bare feet brushing against the cumuli that
is the dance floor of heaven. And a mariachi band, all fiddles
and guitars, ushers them into the Kingdom
where everyone, including Jesus himself, is brown, black,
or some sweet shade in between and the angels' hair
is sweet-smelling and luminous, drenched in
the steady glare of constellations.

INSTRUCTION

I told my students once that cats are bad
because they sneak into dark bedrooms
and suck the breath out of infants. My grandma
told me this, along with how killing daddy longlegs
would make your cows die. She also told me
ghosts and Jesus were real, if I behaved
I'd end up in heaven some day, segregation
was good, store-bought biscuits were for Yankees,
blackberries made the best filling for pastry,
North Carolina sweet potatoes were tastiest,
snakes needed to be dead, Catholics were evil,
rusty barbed wire caused lockjaw, God made
the heavens and the earth in a week,
dogs should never be allowed inside, castor
oil was the cure for any sickness,
skin was meant to be scrubbed
on Sunday mornings, June bugs loved to be tied to strings,
lightning bugs belonged in ball Jars, ladybugs
were a sign of good luck, couches should
be covered by plastic, the radio should
be tuned to the Grand Ole Opry, goats
were mean, cows would kick, chickens would peck
your bare feet, bears roamed the woods,
perch was better fried with cornbread,
and, of course, elves lived in that magic place
where trees meet in the distance
over the highway that leads west to Lynchburg.

How to Keep the Devil Away:

Never open your umbrella inside.
Don't forget to unplug the phone during electric storms.
Don't go outside with wet hair.
Don't swallow watermelon seeds or they'll bloom in your belly.
Don't forget that rain and sun at the same time mean the devil is beating his wife.
Put an acorn on the windowsill to keep lightning out.
Don't touch dead people's hands.
Seeing a crow cross your path is bad luck.
Don't bring eggs in after dark.

Remember: When a snake's head is severed, it will not die until sunset.
The devil can enter your body when you sneeze.

Each Morning I Wake Up Filled with Dreams

and darkness, barely remembering the flutter
of birds, the loud clicking of a clock in another room
that signals there is time passing
in dreams as well as the daylight
I awakened to: Florida summer.
A light rain of mosquitoes.
My little dog eating grass because
her stomach's upset. A quarter moon
already high in the eastern sky
and sunlight burning the fringes
of cumuli. I drink coffee, feeling
the clarity that comes on like a foreign language's
beautiful shadows speaking the past in barns and swallows,
in the brown and white cow kicking its stall
and once kicking my little brother's head. He was only 3

and my grandfather carried him from the barn
back to the house where the Baptist women
gathered around him, my grandmother wiping
away the blood with a kitchen towel as I wondered
at the tiny gash just above his black eyebrow,
a little quarter moon itself without the light.

This happened a long time ago before all the pine
woods were chopped down, before my grandfather
lost his farm, before the big oak in the front yard
was killed by lightning, before my grandma's favorite
calico cat died at 15, before I lost my religion,
discovered Jesus was only a ghost and the Bible
its own book of the dead filled with pestilence and drought,
the sacrifices of lambs and children while
blood flowed knee deep through the streets of Jerusalem.

Fire this time the preachers promised
on Sunday mornings in another world
where cars guzzled gas and flew over
one-lane roads lined with kudzu
and honeysuckle. Sip the horn
of a blooming honeysuckle blossom
and you will be transformed forever,
tricked into believing in a sweetness
that fades like the memory
of the red oaks and chestnuts
flashing by in their green syllables of summer.

These Days

I lie in bed
on our spinning little planet,
imagining fields dim
then brightening. I see
it all, walk each night
the soft dirt road
childhood lay beneath my feet.
I see big and little dippers
fill with dark waters,
watch the night trickle
down in all its tender
mercy: ghosts of Issa
and Basho riding cosmic waves,
Walt Whitman licking
the Milky Way
until his beard glows
vanilla, a billion babies
descending from heaven
in their glory cloaks,
dressed for happiness,
destined for this world,
yes, this world that moans
through its pages, travels
around the sun, flashes
bright glaciers--spinning
revival, spinning wheel,
spinning top, spinning, spinning
spinning. No wonder I'm dizzy

on Florida mornings, awakening
to the monochromatic green
where big squirrels chase
each other up and down
a slash pine, the dog's ears
rising and falling to the branch

thunder of little brown gods,
the sun trickling through palms,
the wind heaving just enough
to jiggle the philodendron leaves.

What Do Men Want? After Kim Addonizio

I want a cherry-red 1965 Mustang
with a manual transmission.
I want to be 18 again
driving through the streets
of a strange place I've never visited.
I want it to be a small town with
one bank, a single grocery store,
and a solitary bar where all the locals
drink their nights away. I want everyone
in the tavern to be a man who's lost something.
I want half of them to be crying into their beer.
I want the other half to be laughing
at the men who are crying—in other words,
I want realism. I want the desperation
that comes from time and booze.
I want a shot of Jim Beam, please, and give
me back those 10 years I wasted working
on that oil pipeline in Nebraska. It was a cold,
shitty job. All the women I met hated me
because I always smelled like smoke and distance.
The only thing I knew to talk about
was the way the daylight retreated
from a landscape that was emptiness,
drought, dust and the hallucinations
of ghost Irishmen building a railroad, dragging
the cottonwood ties to the gravel bed
that mostly wandered west. I want
a different memory filled with carnivals
and circus clowns. I want to ride a Ferris
wheel beneath a star-pierced sky
that is so beautiful, I'll repeat it
seven times. I want the bearded lady
to fall in love with me. I want to have

six bearded children who will become
their own show, complete with fireworks
that go off after they do that thing with the lion.

THE LIKELIHOOD OF DEATH

when standing next to a tall slash pine in a storm can be calculated by dividing the velocity of the lightning bolt by the total number of days you wasted in fourth grade staring at that skinny little girl with the amazing blue eyes, which seemed to glow with the sure knowledge of another world where maybe love was possible and the principal breakfast food was chocolate ice cream. You can also figure out how likely you are to deliver a newborn calf by multiplying the number of dairy farms in your state by the elevation of each farm and then dividing everything by 12. Curious about what happens when you die? Simply put 15 lightning bugs in a jar and ask 15 people if the creatures are called bugs or fireflies. The bug number becomes the numerator and the fly number the denominator in a fraction that must be multiplied by the speed of light.

Once you've reached a final answer to these questions, write it down on lilac-perfumed stationery, buy a tractor and drive west for 59 miles, then bury the answer by the side of the road. If, however, there is roadkill within a mile of your burial, you must fetch the dead creature and gently bury it with your answer. Make sure you cover the grave when you're done so that other contestants may not cheat their way into avoiding death by lightning, delivering calves, or discovering the truth about Heaven and Hell.

Real reality

Once, years ago when my wife was away,
to relieve our loneliness the dog and I watched
"Intervention," a reality TV show in which a family
intervened in the life of a husband and father
who was drinking himself to death,
and praise the lord, halfway through the show
he swore off booze because he finally saw the reality
of his desperate situation, and his wife and daughters
cried tears of happiness, but I knew something was
wrong because there were still 20 minutes left,
plenty of time for another reversal, which came
when the newly sober man found out his liver
was pickled, so the show ended with a picture
of the man, and the date of his death. The dog

and I hated the ending. We wanted the man to live
long and prosper like space travelers who'd been
blessed by Vulcans. In reality there was no happiness,
no long walks on the beach with the grateful family,
no slow-motion montage of birthday parties and christenings,
no final frame of the reformed drunk holding his wife's hand
as they walked into the kitchen on an average morning
and drank coffee and listened to the birds singing in the backyard,
as they talked about the mundane things that make up real
reality: Maxwell House with a little cream and sugar, the broken
ice maker in the freezer, the way the man once noticed there were a few
more wrinkles around his wife's eyes and how that made him happy.

During My Dark City Days

I drank most afternoons in smoke-filled taverns
where men boasted about the sizes of their penises
and played an aggressive kind of pinball that
rocked the machine even as it blipped
and jangled. There was an art
to shaking Sinbad but not so much
that the dreaded "tilt" would appear
ending any chance of barroom domination.
I spent weekday afternoons and evenings
hitting buttons, forcing flippers to whack
steel balls that sometimes brought a chorus
of chimes and bells but more often delivered
the silence that forced me back to a mug
of Old Style, to the high-pitched voices
of all of us trying to speak louder than
the jukebox and the pinball machine, so
that we might at last be heard, and maybe
in that way, somehow loved. I don't go

to bars anymore, so I have no idea
what drunken games the patrons play, but I do
know what happened to me: the smooth
night of drunkenness, that feeling we think
is real love luring me to an unheated storage
room where fallen sirens awaited. I'd see
my breath rush to vapor as I shared
an angel's embrace—angel of bleached blonde
hair, angel with blackened front teeth, angel
who wiggled and smiled and hated me, and
how I loved the hate, the feeling of failure
and sin, which grounded me in a little shame,
which allowed me to feel my heart's
ragged beat as the hours multiplied
until last call: 2 a.m. in the dark
city, occasional buses grinding down Halsted

Street, the moon barely aglow, quartered
in the deep night of a universe that even then
stretched out to unknowable distances like
a road in Iowa splitting cornfields, a sliver
of meaning aiming for Kansas or Minnesota,
finding a thousand lakes or a thousand fields
of golden grain, finding American meaning
beneath a million stars that shone brightly
as if they were still alive. *Chicago, 1981*

Singing to the Night Birds *for Michael Hettich*

Each night at dusk I listen to
the sorrow of a chuck-will's-widow,
goat sucking cousin of the whippoorwill,
whose *whip poor weels* haunt the dog and me
as we walk beneath a Florida night
where the faded constellations
whisper their own sweet nothings
amid bird cry, starlight, the hiss of the dog peeing
on my neighbor's purple Mexican heather.

The dog pees, the stars shine, the bird
sings—and for a moment I wish for this confluence
of sacred things to last forever, and isn't that Big Dipper
the same constellation my grandma showed me in 1959,
and hasn't she been dead from cancer for 30 years?

The dog spins to chase a marsh rabbit that's
already disappeared into a firebush hedge, which earlier
today was filled with butterflies, which earlier
this year were cocooned in a long trance
that always precedes the bright burning
from caterpillar to miracle, symbol of transformation,
spreader of pollen to Florida flowers,
including the five-fisted pentas'
purple and red petals bringing color to the areca's green wall,
burning through the shady darkness, praising, always praising
the light of a world not yet undone.

I Want to Come Back as a Toaster

Crows caw this rainy morning across the St. Augustine
grass and I think of days I played baseball
on green Virginia pastures that often glowed
brighter than the sun. I grew up hearing stories
about my grandpa and uncles, the magnificent home runs they hit
into the stand of red oak trees that complicated center field. By the time
I came along, there were rusty Fords pushed into the shadow of the barn
and in foul ground past third base an occasional appliance listed
a little sideways, ready to someday fall into earth and memory,
to be redeemed by the soil, like all of us. I'd want to come

back as a toaster, red-hot for a few minutes, my innards pulsing
electric wires up and down the dreary slice
of bread, the sometimes body of Christ,
communion on dreary Sundays when the crows
whisper *god is dead* into the buzz of telephone
and power lines that spread the gospel of Microsoft, those
bland verses you would have never found
on a Burma-Shave sign, disappearing in the green
blight of kudzu, the wisdom of *the place for admiring curves
you know, is only at the beauty show* strangled
in the shadow of the valley of a weedy death.
I wonder about the lives of toasters, their histories
of fire and crumbs, of desire and memories of the bland toast
that awaits a slab of butter and maybe a little blackberry
jam that is a poor imitation of the preserves my grandma canned
in Virginia summers so that even the winters might be sweet
with fruit when the holy ghost whispered to the biscuits.

Because Frank Fell Down

When my dad's house caught fire last year
much of my childhood was destroyed: picture
albums and yearbooks, report cards, that
award certificate from sixth grade celebrating
my first-place finish in the 50-yard dash,
and an old tape recording of Neil Armstrong's
first words on the moon.

Much was lost, but my brother salvaged a few
pictures, most taken at my grandpa's farm
in Burkeville, Virginia, revealing the red-brick house
built after the Civil War, a place I've dreamed so often
now the backdrop for a black and white picture
of my mom holding me when I was a baby
as a goat walks by in the background.

My mom was so beautiful then, with her
dark black hair and shy smile. I look
at her eyes and see how much she loved me.
Picture after picture, these tiny testaments
to a perfect love so long ago when a mid-
20th-century sun lit the tobacco fields
and there were still hundreds of acres
of oak and pine covering those Nottoway
County hills. In the late 60s
the land was logged, reduced
to a moonscape. My grandpa's love
of booze accelerated and he coasted
downhill past the grim markers on the road
to alcoholism, smiling the entire way.

I look at pictures and find what was once real.
I look at pictures and see the tangible: love
and barns, the windmill, the rusty pump
that summoned iron-tinted water from

the well, from the Virginia underground
where old gods stirred and stuttered
each evening when the sun left us
alone in the starry darkness of a world
without lights where it did seem as if
God and heaven were close, and that the moon
was closer still, something I could almost
touch before I crawled beneath my grandma's
quilts and dreamed of love and the moon,
of a righteous God protecting us
from any earthly harm.

I have to add that I won that 50-yard dash
in sixth grade only because a kid named Frank, who
was faster than me, slipped at the starting line.
And, by the way, the goat in the background of the picture
with my mom was white with black spots
and a mean son of a bitch.

Broken World

My dad joked with everyone he met,
the cashiers at the grocery store,
the man he bought cigarettes from
at the 7-Eleven, every neighbor who passed
by his ranch style house in Newport News
with its pretty flowers out front. When my
mom went to the nursing home, he joked
with the nurses, the nurses' assistants,
the other patients, and often took
cigarette breaks outside with a man
who'd lost his legs from diabetes
but still smoked his Marlboros
in the little patio on the side of the home
that looked out over some piney woods
filled with robins and cardinals, a little
bit of beauty in that broken world. After his
death I found out how much everyone loved
my dad, how they missed his sense of humor,
the way he talked to everyone in the kind way
of someone who knows how desperate life is
and how the little things sometimes accrue into treasures
of the spirit. Some nights I dream

of the nursing home. Some nights
I try to reassure myself that I am not losing my life,
that others aren't aware of my forgetfulness when I can't
remember the waitress's name at the Mexican restaurant
we went to for years, until the health department closed
them down, until the sad sign appeared on the door:
We will be back soon, which was a wish
that didn't happen and now that storefront
in the ugly mall outside the gated community we hate
is empty and many of the other businesses have left
including the memorabilia shop with the statue of a horse out front
that sold antique guns and swords, the place we laughed at

until it was suddenly gone, like our restaurant, leaving absence
amid the asphalt and almost dead shrubbery of a dying strip mall
in Florida. *Hah, the waitress's name was Flor, and she loved me*
because I gave her huge tips for not correcting my bad Spanish
and laughing at every single one of my jokes. And now

there's no *La Fogata,* and my dad is two years dead. I listen
to country and western songs to remind me of what's important:
family, Jesus, whippoorwills singing across rural dawns
where the morning's sky is a page from
the front matter in Grandma's Bible, King James
version of course, filled with fire,
damnation, salvation, pestilence, and drought.
I think of a thirsty Jesus lost in the desert,
I think of the 100-year-old lady
waiting in her wheelchair by the front door
of the nursing home, begging each
passerby to please take her home.

Kudzu Hymn

I found out at my dad's funeral
for his first job out of high school
he helped plant kudzu along country roads
for the state highway department. They believed
it would anchor the loose soil between
barbed-wire fences and Burma-Shave signs.

These days the green invasive
suffocates entire counties,
obscuring pine trees and billboards, a million
Japanese leaves clinging to vines
that spiral through the quiet countryside,
strangling old barns and abandoned houses
into grey ruins filled with uneasy ghosts.

I wonder what would have happened
if my dad and his fellow workers
had planted haiku instead of kudzu,
if, for decades, little poems bloomed
over pastures and fields, along one-lane roads,
some of them, to this day, gravel-covered
and waiting for the bite of tires
to scatter them into song? What if Issa's
images sparkled in Southern moonlight,
if every creek was a canvas for paintings of birds
and green hills, for the humble frog, the dinner
chicken that clacked happily through a village
where children chased the shadows of cumuli
through bright afternoons? What if Basho's
monk crapped behind an abandoned dairy barn
as he considered humility and the heavy weight
of progress, how sometimes the village fires
obscured the waning moon?

But the kudzu plant grows in leaflets of three:
maybe a hundred thousand acres of poems
have already been written!

Modern Life

To-do list:
hope for a tornado,
hold on tightly to dog,
then follow, follow, follow,
follow the yellow brick road.

Call psychiatrist.
Change drugs?

Why did you make me crazy, dear Lord?
Why do I make sure all my pairs of shoes
are mated before I leave the house?
Why do I check the coffee pot several times,
then every faucet, every light?
Why, even then, do I feel paralyzed
as I walk out into a world of Florida light,
that early morning cacophony
of tree frogs and blue jays
in the miraculous haze of this new day?

Called psychiatrist.
Changed drugs,
then felt so wired I hyperventilated for a week.

Called psychiatrist back.
She said, "Whoops."

And I do hear whooping inside my brain,
a chorus of old dogs longing for heaven
in a beautiful and ragged cascade of barks,
which is not unlike a waterfall in reverse,
the gleaming words headed upstream,
not down into the valley of the shadow,

a place without dogs
that is not without dark,
the very fabric of nightmare,
the truest flotsam of shiver and foam.

Noonday *Duende*

Someone once called it the noonday demon.
I call it this poem, which is sinking down
the page in syllables that frighten me,
an unbeliever in this beautiful land.
Let's call it Florida. I call it this poem
filling with blooming firebush, which,
according to *brujas*, will keep the evil
spirits away. Our house is surrounded
by firebush and the butterflies that glide
among them, but somehow a *duende*
sneaks through the circle each day and grips
my heart with his tiny fist. His fingers
are cold and he sings Granada into my memory
and I see the snowy Sierra Nevada beyond
the Alhambra, and I remember the *Generalife*,
how the fountains spoke Arabic, how bare-
footed ghosts slipped past the night-blooming jasmine,
their eyes bright as mountain stars.

Minus
for Colleen Hettich
...instead of *catkin, cauliflower, chestnut and clover*, today's edition of the (Oxford Junior) dictionary, which is aimed at seven-year-olds...features *cut and paste, broadband and analogue.*

Who cares about elongated clusters
of flowers from willow and birch trees,
who notices the head of cauliflower
with its *white inflorescence meristem*,
who still collects chestnuts to roast on an open fire,
who still rolls happily through fields of clover?
I cut and pasted *white inflorescence meristem*
from Wikipedia, snagged elongated
clusters from dictionary.com, picked chestnuts
and clover from my own memory,
which is filled with green pastures and dark woods.
I think we need to start putting dark woods
back into dictionaries and maybe sending
kids to primitive churches in southern Alabama
where they are forced to handle diamondbacks
in order to find Jesus, so that they might
rise above the mundane chatter of *this world*
and see what's truly holy, and in that moment
of ecstasy, disappear into the sacred,
which is born of snake skin and flowers,
which is the humming howl of creation,
the green fuse, the naked truth
animating serpents, glowing beneath
the magical clover pollinated by bumble
bees, transformed into sweetness,
into nectar that tastes really good on homemade
biscuits, the only kind that children used to eat,
back in the day, back in a time when we'd finish
breakfast and be sent outside until dinner
until a soft dusk spread across the horizon,
which in later years we would define as "twilight,"

which I suppose has now been replaced by Twitter,
which is a proper noun and is not bird singing
in general, those sweet melodies that can't be tweeted,
that spring from the tension in syringeal muscles,
not the outcome of fingers tapping a keyboard.

Beer Aisle Meditation: *Fort Myers, Florida 2018*

I'm buying beer for my wife and I linger too long
checking prices and brands, discovering
that the cost of a six-pack has tripled
in 30 years. I explore all the microbrewery
possibilities until I find my wife's favorite: the Funky Buddha
and imagine being a funky Buddhist wiggling my butt a little
during meditation. Maybe I'd write haiku
that sounded best with a jazz band but right now
I'm looking at the domestic brews and wondering
if it would be bad to try the non-alcoholic brand
and then I'm thinking, maybe just one bottle of the alcoholic
persuasion, but since I'm personally of the alcoholic
persuasion, one beer might lead to more
like a single cloud becoming a week
of stormy weather. Weather is a feckless

tribute to wind and cloud and heat and cold.
The atmosphere is thin but still manages to hold in
the storms, then the calm in-betweens when sheep graze
on cool pastures outside Edinburgh and the ghosts
of Viking warriors pose for selfies in the imaginations
of heather and mountains purpled with destiny. A long,

long time ago, I got drunk in a bar in Edinburgh. There was
a man playing a fiddle. The joint offered good Chinese food
and the beer was served at room temperature. I can still see
the varnished bar, the universe of glittering bottles behind it,
and the happiness I felt, knowing this place would never run
out of booze and I could drink here until the end of history,
which is simply that moment when the foamy glass blurs,
when the bartender is speaking a language that might be
Sanskrit or Norwegian or maybe the cold syllables of Inuit
spoken to a dying English sailor. It is simply that moment

when reality softens and the desire to walk out of the bar

meets the inertia of a body so deep in its dream of booze
standing up seems impossible. All those years ago, I did stand up
and somehow walked back to the hotel on Princess Street
where I collapsed on a bed in a room without a bathroom
so when it was time to throw up, I stumbled down the hall
found a toilet and looked into the mirror where all meaning was lost.

All these years later while roaming the beer aisle
I see the meaning of English words shaped into names for fancy beers.
It's been over 30 years since I've felt foam on my mustache.
It's been 20 years since I've had a mustache. I put the Funky Buddhas
into my shopping cart next to the ice cream I substitute for alcohol,
each one a quick fix on a cellular level, each one a sweet desire that
calms my hunger for a moment. Ice cream will not kill me as quickly,
however, and in the years that may remain I will not spin out of control
from too much Heath Bar Crunch. I go home and that night

I dream of the beer aisle. It goes on forever from Virginia to California.
As far as I can see, there are bottles of beer stretching to the blue Pacific,
it's a Manifest Destiny of sainted brews. There are 3,000 miles
of highways and towns with taverns where patrons drink beer. There are
breweries next to great rivers where enormous stainless-steel vats
froth with hops, grain, and yeast. I dream of swimming in a beer vat,
of drunk-drowning my way into the afterlife. I dream of angels
dressed like barmaids, of Hank Williams on the jukebox. I dream
of falling asleep forever on the bosom of a stranger who strokes
my hair and whispers sweetly to me as I forget who I was,
who I am, whatever it was I'd wanted to be. I dream until the dream
dissolves like the cold fog on a beer glass that becomes part of the greater
air, that becomes the weather, becomes the very clouds that will one day
rain and rain again into rivers that roll into the sea.

In memory's blue sedan,

it was almost as if time had dissolved
and I could hear my great aunt Sarah praising
the sweet honeysuckle-entwined
barbed wire that lined the dark
country road. After all,
there was moonlight and that whole
world gleamed in the way only dreams
can. I never talked to Sarah
in my waking life. I knew her only
through stories my mom and grandma
told me after they visited her at the asylum
in Williamsburg where she'd been committed
after trying to flag down a biplane in 1930. She wanted
the pilot to take her to Jesus. Because heaven

is real in the way that moonlight is real, indivisible
fabric of yellow light. Because it won't bend or
tear when you run your hands through it, because
it has no taste or sound, because the wind can't
ripple Paradise the way it does Sarah's grey hair, because
the front windows are down in this dream,

I wonder what's so crazy about wanting to reach Jesus
by airplane? What's silly about talking to Him in the kitchen
the way Sarah used to? My grandma said she even asked
the Savior how much flour to put in the biscuits each morning
and thanked Him for the delicious bounty of fresh eggs and fatback.

When Sarah tried to flag down the biplane,
she waved one of her prize-winning quilts
from the State Fair in Richmond. I wonder
if the pilot looked down, saw that little square
juxtaposed against the green fields that surrounded her?
I wonder if pilots in those early days
thought of themselves as gods, risen

from the earth, looking down at the trembling
beauty of an older world where each night
the darkness shaped pastures, forests, and fields
into a long black, while here and there a town
gleamed brightly like a constellation
at the edge of a heaving sea? Narrative

fails to get back to the sound of one engine
thrumming through that distant night
when I imagine Aunt Sarah sleeping
beneath the Savior's picture, His hands
clasped in prayer, humming little Jesus
wisdoms into her sleep. *Blessed are*
the meek for they shall inherit the earth.

Jesse Millner's poems have appeared in *River Styx, Pearl, The Prose Poem Project, Gravel, The Florida Review, Wraparound South, The Best American Poetry 2013* and other literary magazines. He has published seven poetry chapbooks and two full-length collections, *The Neighborhoods of My Past Sorrow* (winner of bronze medal in 2010 Florida Book Awards) and *Dispatches from the Department of Supernatural Explanation* (Kitsune Books, 2012). Jesse has received writing fellowships at Fundacion Valparaiso in Mojacar, Spain, and at the U-Cross Foundation in Clearmont, Wyoming. He currently teaches writing courses at Florida Gulf Coast University in Fort Myers, Florida.

HYSTERICAL BOOKS

www.ingramcontent.com/pod-product-compliance
Lightning Source LLC
Chambersburg PA
CBHW020659300426
44112CB00007B/453